Deep Thoughts

James Dean Rivera

Copyright© 2020 James Dean Rivera
ISBN: 978-81-949003-6-8

First Edition: 2020
Rs. 200/-

Cyberwit.net
HIG 45 Kaushambi Kunj, Kalindipuram
Allahabad - 211011 (U.P.) India
http://www.cyberwit.net
Tel: +(91) 9415091004 +(91) (532) 2552257
E-mail: info@cyberwit.net

Printed at Repro India Limited.

Contents

Curvaceous Women 5

Broke (No Hope) 6

No Longer 7

A Perfect World 8

Success And Jealousy 9

I Am A Man 10

We're In This Love Together 11

9 To 5 12

He Can't Love You 13

Still A Boy 14

Back To 17 15

Lies and Deception 16

I Rise 17

Rise And Grind 18

The Fire Burns 20

This Could Have Been You 21

Insecure Lady 22

To Chase My Dream 23

Quit Talking Keep On Walking 24

Built To Last 25

Did I Mention 27

Why Women Cheat 28

You Are Worthy 29

My Real Nightmare 30

One Woman Man 32

Good Intentions Gone Bad 33

The Sands Of Time 34

Controlled Society 35

That Time Has Passed 36

Love Not Hate 37
World Falling Apart 38
Stop Hating Yourself 39
Blinded By Love 40
My Biggest Regret 42
Dear Surviving World 43

Curvaceous Women

What you call fat I call curvaceous,
More to love and thick in the right places,
They hold such big personalities,
God created thick women accordingly.

Thick thighs that mesmerize,
Curves that hypnotize,
Thick in the waist,
And ass all over the place.

Most thick women are never insecure,
They know us men love them for sure
For us a skinny woman never does the trick,
We get turned on by a woman that's thick.

There's no use in fat shaming,
The negativity that you're aiming,
They'll laugh and laugh at your bony ass,
Some of them will even steal your man.

I love thick women always,
Skinny women I'm never satisfied no way,
I'm glad my lady is thick and curvaceous,
She is the love of my life thank goodness gracious.

Broke (No Hope)

I'm tired of feeling broke,
Tired of being in a downward slope,
They say money is the root of all evil,
But we all need money let's face it people.

The rent is too high utility costs soar,
Food and gas prices go up even more,
The overall cost of living becomes too much,
Paycheck to paycheck it's not enough.

Some people resort to unethical methods,
They Rob stores do pyramid schemes things that get them arrested,
Some will do things the honest way even work 2 jobs,
They pay their taxes it's better to follow the law.

Some people are homeless in desperate need of hope,
Down and out no hope on the horizon broke,
Everywhere you turn it seems someone is begging,
For hope on the horizon there's no telling.

But I know I have hope,
I know soon I won't be broke,
I'll be richer than in my wildest dreams,
Hope is in the horizon for me.

No Longer

When I was young I was shy,
No one liked me and I never knew why,
I was different from the others and quiet,
Could Have changed but I never tried it.

I was always picked on cuz of my tight clothes,
Stood back did nothing is what I chose,
I just let people physically and verbally abuse me,
But to cheat on tests they would use me.

No girl seemed to want me,
Not the pretty ones or even the ones that were ugly,
I was frustrated I never understood why,
Couldn't figure it out no matter how I tried.

I tried too hard to fit in but I always stood out,
Tried to be cool but was too much of a lout,
But one day when I stopped trying things suddenly changed,
The problems no longer seemed to be within range.

I started talking more to people,
No longer did I feel like I was feeble,
I no longer was a scared little boy,
No longer could anyone treat me like a toy.

I evolved into more of a fighter,
No longer was my life going to feel dire,
I am now a man who takes shit from no one,
Those days are now gone.

A Perfect World

In a perfect world nothing would go wrong,
In a perfect world we would all get along,
No wars no nation divided,
Come join the party you are all invited.

The rent won't go high and utility costs won't soar,
Everyone will be prosperous there will be no poor,
Crime will be non-existent and the world will be safe,
Paradise will be in your own backyard no need for an escape.

You can have multiple wives or any riches you seek,
You can have anything in your wildest dreams within reach,
Cheat on your wife or they neighbors wife no problem,
No failures success will always blossom.

But although what a life that would be,
We all have to face reality,
For a perfect world doesn't exist,
And almost nothing in reality co exists.

Success And Jealousy

What's wrong with success,
Or striving for the best,
Too much jealousy in many circles,
Too many people who are hurtful.

They not in your shoes,
Pace around singing the blues,
Jealous of those who have succeeded,
They feel so depleted.

They complain they don't have a big bank account,
Live crappy with debts continuing to mount,
Wondering why they don't live in success,
Wallowing in pity and getting stressed.

They're not like people who grind and work hard,
Lazy and complainers is what they are,
The green eye of jealousy it's taken over,
Continue to try to make people feel lower and lower.

It's not people's fault they have success,
It's not their fault that they strive for the best,
Other people can be in their shoes,
But be jealous Bitch and moan they choose.

There's nothing wrong with success,
It doesn't have to be in excess,
It takes hard work and a strong pace,
You have to find success, success does not wait.

I Am A Man

I am a man,
A Man is what I am,
I am a human being,
A person with meaning.

I am not a boy or a slave
I did not live in a cave,
Nor am I unintelligent,
Not now or even then.

I'm outspoken I never bite my tongue,
I fear no one and I do not run,
I always speak my mind I am opinionated,
Whatever I think I say it.

Don't care if those I offend,
Cross me and I will defend,
I'm the nicest guy but your worst enemy,
Try your best not to Fuck with me.

And acknowledge me for who I am,
I am not your slave Bitch I am a man,
If you can't see that then to hell with you,
Enough explaining myself I'm through.

We're In This Love Together

We're in this love together,
We're in this love forever,
The way up is the path,
Our love is sure to last.

Nothing can stop us at this point,
King and queen for ourselves we can anoint
We will rule our castle,
And won't face no hassle.

We will be married in a beach on a garden,
And a family we will be starting,
Have a girl and name her Jenna,
Take her to Spain Paris Rome and Vienna.

We will always be traveling,
No problems unraveling,
The family that loves one another,
Well vacation every summer.

We will grow old together,
Still be in love with each other,
Never falling victim to each other's negativity,
We will be happy we sure will be.

9 To 5

I dream of a life,
A life of no more 9 to 5,
Where money is no longer an issue,
Where success always continues.

No more answering to bosses that are dumb,
Or working with a bunch of incompetent bums,
Being miserable on a daily basis,
The agony I'll no longer have to face it.

I'm not asking for a life of luxury,
Just to live life more colorfully,
Carefree more accomplished less worried,
A life fit for me more worthy.

No more paycheck to paycheck,
No more struggling to pay the rent,
No more working with those with more failures than success,
Fuck it I know I'll soon be better than the rest.

I can't see myself struggling breaking my ass till I'm 62,
That's not the life I'm willing to choose,
No longer will my life be a 9 to 5,
That life soon will have to die.

He Can't Love You

He Can't love you what part don't you understand?
He Can't love you because he can't be a man,
He Can't offer you no love of comfort,
All he can do is freak you under the covers.

He Can't offer you no flowers,
Maybe he can only offer you golden showers,
He Can't take you on a night on the town,
Netflix and chill that's what's going down.

He has other women in tow,
He may even have guys on the low,
Faithfulness is not in his DNA,
He ain t gonna love you no way.

He will break your heart and leave you confused,
Your trust he will continue to abuse,
Drain your time your money everything,
Leave you barely hanging on a string.

He's not worth it find someone else,
Don't keep on fooling yourself,
There's better men out there,
He Can't love you he don't care

Still A Boy

He's a young man who's successful,
Has a job that's not so stressful,
Wears Armani suits and drives a Mercedes,
And married to a beautiful lady.

He has everything most people can't buy,
People almost look at him like a rich guy,
Want to be like him in every way possible,
But most couldn't do it if they was able.

He may not have no baby drama,
But he still lives with his mama,
Banging other ladies he's in contact with,
Bang them and leave them that's it.

Wife talks about him like he's the sweetest thing on earth,
Her stupid ass don't know that he's a fucking jerk,
All the women the extra phone he keeps,
He may even have Std's.

I hope she discovers his secrets and leaves him to burn,
I hope for him it'll be a lesson learned,
He can have all the expensive shirts and cars to enjoy,
But he's not a man he is still just a boy.

Back To 17

If I was 17 things would have been different,
I would have been less nice and less considerate,
Less tolerant of negativity surrounding me,
And fought with a vengeance the problems that compounded me.

I would have had more confidence,
My life would have meant more prominence,
Would have better faced my fears,
And stand up to my peers.

I'd destroy the power of the teenager,
And I wouldn't be no peace maker,
Raise hell run them out of town,
They'd be no longer able to throw down.

I'd get the girl and become more popular,
Life wouldn't feel so monitored,
Join in on extracurricular activities,
Be invited to all the parties and festivities.

I would have had a prom date,
Lost my virginity I wouldn't have had to wait,
Everything would have been perfect,
The good life it would have been worth it.

Lies and Deception

Lies and deceit are all around me,
Lies and Deception are 2 bad surroundings,
There seems no point or end,
People are your enemies but act like your friends.

It seems so hard to believe,
People seem good but intend to deceive,
You don't know Who to trust they're all targets,
The deception seems so hard to forget.

Deceit and Deception over and over,
The chances of a good friend is like a 4 leaf clover,
It's hard these days to find good friends,
And even when you do it's bad in the end.

But you should not let friends determine fate,
Make choices for the best sooner than late,
Lies are like a diseased infection,
Life is full of deceit and Deception.

I Rise

There's a place I've come to know,
It is an anchor for my soul,
When everything seems to fail,
At the end all turns up well.

From the ashes I Rise,
Failure is not something to live by,
Victory is always won,
And the problems I overcome.

No more sorrow no more pain,
Nothing can be the same,
I will be a success,
I can't expect nothing less.

I will be rich and have everything I dream of,
It's what my hopes lean on,
The money the cars starting a family,
There can be triumph after tragedy.

Everything will fall into place,
And not a moment too late,
I'm sure it will be that time,
The time that I Rise.

Rise And Grind

I wake up on a Monday,
Monday is always mundane,
Can't sit around looking at the clouds,
Can't live my day in doubt.

I wake up on a Tuesday,
Always feels like a blues day,
But can't keep that on my mind,
Still got to get up rain or shine.

I wake up on a Wednesday
It's no always the best day,
But it's hump day the middle of the week,
Still got to get up on my feet.

I wake up on a Thursday,
Confidence isn't always bursting,
But success is around the corner
Got to still keep things in order.

I wake up on a Friday,
Just like everyday it's my day,
Got to keep on going,
No opportunities blowing.

No work Saturday or Sunday but still I rise,
I continue to keep my eyes on the prize,
Take an off day that's never,
Still have to keep my plans together.

No matter what I do,
No matter how the day goes thru,
Dreams don't sleep so I always rise,
I continue to rise and grind.

The Fire Burns

The Fire Burns,
There's no one but her,
She's here to stay,
I'm keeping it that way.

I love her forever,
That won't be severed,
Our love continues to go strong,
Nothing else can go wrong.

It's been like an eternity,
Since she's been here with me,
God brought us here,
To live in happiness not tears.

The obstacles we face we battle,
We are never rattled,
And we both have each other covered,
We both have each other.

The Love will always be there,
There's passion in the air,
No questions or concerns,
The Fire Burns.

This Could Have Been You

This could have been you,
But you chose not to commit,
This Could Have Been You,
But your heart wasn't in it.

You could have had it all,
But self doubt hit your soul,
Too blind to see opportunity,
No wonder it did not work out with me.

We could have been on vacation,
Great memories we'd be making,
Fell in love with each other madly,
Got married and started a family.

But you were a girl in a woman's body,
Your thinking was always shoddy,
Never giving love a chance,
Not even sex or a bit of romance.

Still living with your mother at thirty three,
Had a curfew home at 8 you had to be,
I cheated on and never regretted it once,
You were a virgin plain and never fun.

I'm glad we broke up via text that day,
I found a lady who loves me in so many ways,
We're in a relationship and so in love,
This Could Have been you but you can't grow up.

Insecure Lady

Have you looked at yourself in the mirror lately?
You're so naturally beautiful and shapely,
No makeup or anything artificially needed,
You're definitely more than just decent.

You don't need no improvement,
Any sort would be so fucking stupid,
From your bright skin to your curvy body,
You look so sexy to me.

Your hair like cascades of waterfalls,
Eyes so bright it got me in awe,
With or without glasses you look great,
Your round ass big tits everything you always amaze.

Maybe you don't feel the same,
Everyone has one of those days,
You wake up not feeling as vibrant as you should,
To feel more vibrant and alive you should.

But believe me you're selling yourself short,
You say you not as pretty but you are and more,
I know many people would agree,
I also know they would believe me.

I hope you can look in the mirror and look past your insecurities,
And a beautiful lovely lady you'll be able to see,
Because you're much more beautiful than you think you are,
You are a gorgeous work of art.

To Chase My Dream

When I wake up I have three choices,
One makes sense and one is pointless,
Either go back to sleep and dream my dreams,
Or wake up and choose the dreams I want for me.

The motivation is Always to succeed,
And to also highly achieve
Still not sell myself short,
Failure is not an option or a resort.

It is no time to stay in the clouds
Neither is there any time for droughts,
Gotta continue to get mine because no one else will,
There is not a moment for time to stand still.

My bank account and hopes are increasing
Insecurities and self doubt are decreasing,
No time to fall back,
No dreams will fade to black.

It's a brand new day and a brand new year,
And I have everything in full gear,
I will continue chasing my dreams,
I will not put all my dreams to sleep.

Quit Talking Keep On Walking

Y'all should quit talking,
And keep on walking,
You both know how Y'all feel,
Got to learn how to deal.

He's no longer by your side,
The secrets he tries to hide,
All the cheating all the lies,
Y'all need to say your final goodbyes.

Leave him anywhere hell leave him in a train station,
Don t make him continue testing you patience,
He's like the tiger that never changes his stripes,
He'll continue to show bark but never any bite.

Just like a turd is always a turd,
He will never keep his word,
A promise is not a promise without being fulfilled,
With him there's no moving forward time stands still.

He will continue to bang other wom2n behind your back,
His heart isn't pure it's full of black,
Don t join him for the ride keep on walking,
Y'all need to move on stop talking.

Built To Last

Did you wonder where this was going,
It was going to be great without us knowing,
The Love that we would eventually share,
We wouldn't have thought this was reality if we dared.

Not after what we both went through again and again,
Years of heartbreak and suffering worse than the mets and the jets,
Seems like victory was nonexistent only the agony of defeat,
The shining star was so far it could never be reached.

After years of being cheated on and lied to,
After many partners we said goodbye to,
It was time for a change in direction,
We had to travel far to finally enter our destination.

For me no more women with EBT cards multiple kids and phat asses,
For you no more men who couldn't keep their dick in their pants,
No more kissing a women with breath like Newports and forties,
For you no more men that treated u like a side dish or only wanted to get naughty.

It was time to change our approaches,
Get rid of these clowns who were like cockroaches,
Find and everlasting love that would be timeless,
And escape from the valley of the mindless.

It's great to be waking up next to u every morning,
And our love continues to be soaring,
Fuck all of our exes they can t have what we have,
Happy anniversary my love we are forever built to last

Did I Mention

I told you I am a man,
A man is what I am,
Bombastic and outspoken,
Hardly ever broken.

Did I also mention that I'm a lover and a fighter,
That I don't do all nighters,
That I don't need materialistic things,
I wear my emotions on my sleeve.

I am a supporter of all walks of life,
Race, gender, creed all are friends of mine,
I am not into cliques,
Cliques are for kids.

I love all types of music except country and opera,
I believe in revenge but I also believe in karma,
I will go anywhere with my fiancée she is my heart,
Even if it is Antarctica.

I will not change to conform to no one's standards,
I want to be rich one day but never pampered,
Continue to be me and live life by my own rules,
Stay to myself and stay true.

So if there was anything else you did not understand,
Ask questions, don't be afraid to ask,
I am who I am just wanted to bring that to your attention,
In case there was something I did not mention.

Why Women Cheat

Why do you think women cheat?,
What are the reasons you think it might be?
There are many reasons why she is cheating,
Her heart is broken and needs healing.

Could be from lack of communication,
Significant other is not supportive and there is no relation,
She is bored and looking for a spark,
And she finds another guy perfect for the part.

She may or may not have her man in her heart,
But she needs to fill a void when things fall apart,
Man gets too caught up with life,
Woman is forgotten no longer feels it is right.

Or there could be other reasons,
Like man cheated on her and she's still seething,
So she exacts her revenge,
Can't get mad what was he supposed to expect?

Some women are also sex fiends,
But they too have needs,
And if they are not met,
Cheating is what you'll expect.

She's not going to continue feeling ignored and neglected,
Underappreciated and disrespected,
Cause like I'll say one more time Women have needs,
And if they're not met they will cheat.

You Are Worthy

You are worthy of true love,
You are my love,
Not his or her love,
My love.

You are my priority,
That's how it should always be,
Forgiving you when no one else can't,
I am your fiancé your future husband.

When you feel darkness swallowing you,
When you feel bad vibes following you,
There's something I'll always say to remind you,
The truth, the real truth.

This is not to boost your ego and hide your pain,
This is to take you out of the dark place in which you've re-
mained,
The past should not define you because you see,
You are love and you are worthy.

My Real Nightmare

I used to cut the pain and the world as well,
How could I survive when all I knew was hell,
My world was falling apart and my life was in decay,
If only this reality could have faded away.

My nightmares wasn't Freddy Kruger or Chucky,
I never had nightmares in my sleep I was lucky,
It was in real life during school hours,
I was bullied, made fun of and had no power.

Blue skies and sunshine felt like darkness and rain,
No matter the weather I felt so much pain,
Felt like I did not belong in this society,
Felt so different from the others had so much anxiety.

The pain lingered on through time,
Felt so alone and had no one on my side,
Felt nothing good would come my way,
Never had happiness to keep me at bay.

The pain went on and on for years,
The nightmares continued to up my fears,
No one in sight maybe I should end myself I thought,
But soon that became an afterthought.

For I rose from adversity and gained more confidence,
Stood up to people and became an optimist,
My nightmares appeared to come to an end,
I felt like I slayed more than a dragon.

No more being bullied or ostracized,
That old me had come and died,
It was the beginning of a new era, a new dawn,
Happiness finally appeared and darkness finally gone.

One Woman Man

I'm no longer in need of a one night stand,
I'm a one woman man,
No need for meaningless night caps,
Blinded by what's between her legs and getting sidetracked.

No need to fill a void that still needs filling,
No need to be in a relationship that's unfulfilling,
Those days we're long gone and not even missed,
Because when I found my true love, everything switched.

I used to believe love was just in movies,
And it was fake and meant nothing to me,
Then when I met my true love it no longer felt like make believe,
I found a woman who loves me faithfully.

It was no longer one woman to the next,
It was no longer a relationship to regret,
This became a miracle that I never expected,
And to cheat I'm no longer tempted.

I learned to love and be faithful,
I've learned to be caring and be grateful,
Love no longer has to be fake,
With my fiancée, I found someone great.

The past will stay in the past,
Turned my player card long ago and not going back,
And she will be my forever partner that is the plan,
I'm a one woman man.

Good Intentions Gone Bad

It started out as a game,
A game played every day,
Playfully we would tease each other,
Even have some fun under the covers,

My intentions was good,
To show I cared like a good man should,
But she seemed to take it too far,
She wanted too much and she broke my heart.

She played me like a piano from hell,
She never treated me well,
Did not return my phone calls all the time,
And soon our relationship came to die.

We would have been better off just messing around,
That way none of this would have went down,
We we're much better off,
It was a mistake falling in love.

I had good intentions but they were bad,
It turned into a bad experience I shouldn't have had,
Never show love to those who wouldn't give it back,
Because sooner or later it disappears to black.

The Sands Of Time

The sands of time are running low,
Soon it'll be the end of all I know,
And as this moment draws near,
Everything seems less clear.

But I have an opportunity to do everything over again,
And to ensure my life will not end,
To undo past mistakes which thank God is not any committed crines,
And change the sands of time.

But of course in life you can't take anything back,
I must continue to move forward and move on track,
Although the sands of time may be running low,
I must make the best of the life I know.

Controlled Society

We live in a controlled society,
Who does it benefit? Neither you or me,
Were trained to work like slaves day after day,
Work day after day till were old and gray.

We are trained to get good grades and get a good job with benefits,
And most people will do it just for the hell of it,
They say the best way to best way to progress is to move up,
Get in a better position become your own boss,

But the problem is you're never your own boss,
Most people don't realize this and they're so lost,
The working life is not as glamorous as it seems,
It's all just one big pyramid scheme.

We step over people trying to reach the top,
Thinking we had this career on lock,
But you still have someone to answer to and you can still get fired,
A job is a cutthroat business no sympathy required.

Having your own business is the best option,
Soon the way we've been trained will be forgotten,
No more working for a boss no one to answer to,
Soon those days will be through.

It's time to stop being a slave to a job or a career,
Take the leap take risks face fears,
No more corporate ladders to climb,
It's time to take control of our lives.

That Time Has Passed

I thought you were one of a kind,
But I must have been out of my mind,
Went through a lot of bumps with you,
Thought we had a love so beautiful.

You were the prettiest lady I ever met,
But that was then and our time I forgot,
You were just a pretty face,
No personality, just ass all over the place.

Yes your beauty did knock me off my feet,
Yes the taste of your lips was so sweet,
You wasn't as good in bed as I thought,
We had more problems than I bargained for.

And it eventually reached its end,
There was a better woman I was able to find,
You never became the best I ever had,
It was long ago that time has passed.

Love Not Hate

Hate is everywhere but don't let it consume you,
Hate is everywhere far right groups will recruit you,
But as it's been said love conquers all,
Love makes for a better world.

Love is powerful love is healing,
It's not a gamble love is dealing,
Not even with marriage or starting a family,
Things will fall together if love is meant to be.

Hate only breaks bonds and starts wars,
Teaches people to throw love out the door,
That it is ok to hate everyone of all different races,
Hate is such a bad influence in many ways.

Never be influenced by the problem that is hate,
Try turning your life into something great,
Love will conquer hate and hate will fail miserably,
Have love in your heart and you will be rewarded exponentially.

World Falling Apart

World falling apart,
People taking it hard,
Panic ensues like nel
And it continues to soar.

It's like a real life The Happening or Bird Box,
Who is outside well not a lot,
The city that never sleeps is now in silence,
Not a time I can remember seeing mostly everything so lifeless.

No movies, no Broadway shows,
No going to bars or restaurants, business is slow,
No sports events, not even march madness,
People are out of work limited money and food it's sadness.

If only there was a solution,
To curtail this unwanted intrusion,
For essentials we don't have to have no quarrels,
And everything can go back to normal.
To go back to our normal lives in the fresh air,
To enjoy the sun, the blue skies, flowers growing everywhere,
This panic and fear for our lives is not useful,
Return to the simple joy that made our lives fruitful.

Stop Hating Yourself

Stop hating yourself,
You're not worse than anyone else,
Give yourself a compliment once in a while,
Always walk with grace and style.

Buy yourself a lobster dinner,
Walk around like a winner,
Wear something sexy whether or not you're alone,
Pleasure yourself while you're home.

Listen to your favorite songs,
Wear a Victoria Secret thong,
Eat some ice cream,
Treat yourself like a queen.

You can even sleep naked,
Your body is sacred,
You will spend the rest of your life with you,
Acknowledge yourself because you're beautiful.

Think of yourself as always blessed,
You have a lot to look forward to and you're all set,
You should always love yourself and be kind,
You're rich with beauty and like a fine wine.

Blinded By Love

I was blinded by love,
Had too much of a crush,
Never saw the real you,
I thought our love was true.

In return I lost myself,
Should have been with someone else,
But it was you I chose,
And you wasn't as precious as a rose.

What was the reason for this?
Why were you such a bitch?
You shattered my heart and broke my dreams,
From the start you never loved me.

It was all lies,
Why did this take long to be realized ,
You gave me clues but I did not pay attention,
We never had a chance to go further that you did mention.

Eventually you left me for another man and gave your love to
him,
Your body mind soul everything seemingly in a whim,
You should have had that with me,
And it was hard to cope with sadly.

You barely felt any remorse,
You flaunted how much you loved him more,

He had a car and yall went all over town,
Snuck him to your parents house and had sex when they weren't
around.

But that just proved what a liar you were,
You never treated me with any worth,
Unlike him you played with my vulnerability,
At no point did you ever want me.

But at the end it wasn't worth holding on to the past,
The hurt I experienced thankfully did not last,
My biggest battle is no longer being fought,
I moved on and you are now a distant thought.

My Biggest Regret

Not leaving her for another man was my biggest regret,
For a long time it was something I would never forget,
Even after all the relationships I still lingered,
The pain for a long time never withered.

I know we would have been a perfect match,
It may have not been the best relationship that I ever had,
But it would have been better than the one that I was with,
It would have been more worth it.

We would have actually went out on dates,
There would be no chance to forsake,
I would have lost my virginity sooner,
It would have been a less stressful future.
But I chose to stay with her instead,
Knowing I'd never have my chance with her in bed,
Holding out hope that something would change,
But that change never came.

She kept toying with my emotions,
She only pretended to show emotion,
But she never did it with me and I was still a virgin,
That chance for love and lust I continued searching.

I could have had it better with the other lady,
But I didn't and for years it drove me crazy,
It was so hard to forget,
Still my biggest regret.

Dear Surviving World

We will overcome this crisis,
We will survive this,
With a strong immune system and faith,
We will not let this seal our fate.

We will be allowed to travel and walk in parks again,
The restrictions will be lifted by then,
There will be no more social distancing,
We can relive great moments that we been missing.

No more lockdown or quarantine,
The regular way of life will be redeemed,
You can once again walk amongst the crowds,
Going to bars and restaurants will be allowed.

Most people will still die after this is over,
For most it will bring people closer and closer,
For most it will take time to recover,
For many a new life will be discovered.

Dear Surviving World, we got this!!!!!!!!

www.ingramcontent.com/pod-product-compliance
Lightning Source LLC
LaVergne TN
LVHW092035190726
843493LV00002B/688